Cambridge English Readers

....

Level 3

Series editor: Philip Prowse

Strong Medicine

Richard MacAndrew

CAMBRIDGE
UNIVERSITY PRESS

CAMBRIDGE UNIVERSITY PRESS
Cambridge, New York, Melbourne, Madrid, Cape Town, Singapore, São Paulo

Cambridge University Press
The Edinburgh Building, Cambridge CB2 2RU, UK

www.cambridge.org
Information on this title: www.cambridge.org/9780521693936

First published 2006

Richard MacAndrew has asserted his right to be identified as the Author of
the Work in accordance with the Copyright, Design and Patents Act 1988.

Printed in India by Thomson Press (India) Limited

A catalogue record for this publication is available from the British Library

ISBN-13 978-0-521-69393-6 paperback
ISBN-10 0-521-69393-4 paperback

ISBN-13 978-0-521-69394-3 paperback plus 2 audio CDs
ISBN-10 0-521-69394-2 paperback plus 2 audio CDs

No character in this work is based on any person living or dead. Any resemblance to an
actual person or situation is purely accidental.

*With thanks to all the practitioners working for the Parkinson's Recovery Project,
and especially to Chris Ells for his support, advice and, not least, his appreciation of
the music of Jerry Garcia.*

Contents

Characters

Deborah Spencer: an American doctor of Chinese medicine
Mark Latto: a British doctor
Tony Martinez: a detective in the Santa Cruz Police
Sylvia Koning: worked with Deborah Spencer
Ray Molinaro: worked with Deborah Spencer
Matthew Crocker: works at Keiffenheim Laboratories
Max: works for Matthew Crocker

Author's note

The alternative treatment for Parkinson's Disease described in this story is based on the work of the Parkinson's Recovery Project in Santa Cruz, California, to which a percentage of the royalties from this work is being donated. For more information about their treatment procedures visit http://www.pdrecovery.org

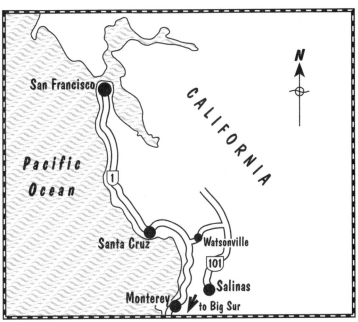

San Francisco

CALIFORNIA

Pacific Ocean

1

Santa Cruz

Watsonville

101

Salinas

Monterey

to Big Sur

N

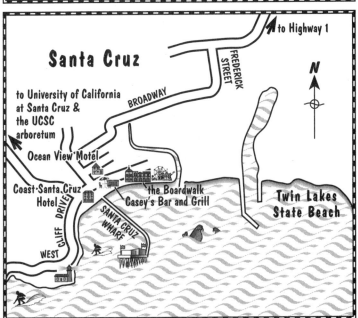

Santa Cruz

to Highway 1

FREDERICK STREET

to University of California at Santa Cruz & the UCSC arboretum

BROADWAY

Ocean View Motel

Coast Santa Cruz Hotel

CLIFF DRIVE

SANTA CRUZ WHARF

WEST

the Boardwalk

Casey's Bar and Grill

Twin Lakes State Beach

N

Chapter 1 *A death in Santa Cruz*

Mark Latto stopped and looked up at the white-painted wooden house on West Cliff Drive. There are many houses like this along the coast of California, many houses like this in Santa Cruz. But this one was different: there was a police car parked on the road outside. A police car outside a house doesn't always mean there's trouble inside, but Latto felt the hairs on the back of his neck stand up. Something wasn't right. He walked towards the front door. As he did so, it was opened by a mountain of a man, at least two metres tall, almost as wide as the door, and wearing the dark blue of the Santa Cruz Police.

'Yes?' asked the police officer in a slow American voice.

'I'm here to see Deborah Spencer,' began Latto. 'She's expecting me.'

'And who are you?'

'My name's Mark Latto. I'm a doctor. I've come over from Britain to see her.'

'Well, you'd better come in, Dr Latto,' said the police officer, stepping back from the door to let Latto in. 'I'm afraid I've got some bad news for you. Ms Spencer was found dead early this morning.'

'Oh no!' Latto put a hand up to his mouth. 'How terrible!'

'Yes,' continued the police officer, 'so I'm afraid you won't get to see her. However, a detective will be along here in a few minutes and he may want to have a talk with you.'

'Detective?' asked Latto. 'Are you saying …?'

'I'm not saying anything, Dr Latto,' said the police officer, looking Latto straight in the eye. 'I'm just asking you to take a seat in that room.' He nodded at an open door on the right. 'Someone will be with you shortly.'

Latto found himself in a light airy sitting room, with a large window looking out over the sea. He put his sunglasses down on a small coffee table and looked out of the window. It was a lovely sunny March day. West Cliff Drive was busy with joggers and people walking their dogs. Further out he could see Santa Cruz Wharf beginning to open up for the day. A van was taking food and drink to one of the restaurants at the end of the wharf. A few men and women were fishing from the side. And although it was early in the year, there were one or two tourists walking along the wharf, looking into the shop windows.

Latto was tall with dark brown hair and blue eyes. He was wearing a light-coloured jacket and trousers and a light blue shirt. He turned and looked at himself in the mirror on the wall. Although he was in his early thirties, he looked older. It was probably tiredness, he thought. It was ten in the morning here in California, but his body was still on British time. He sat in a yellow armchair near the window and closed his eyes. Time passed.

*   *   *

'Dr Latto?' said a voice.

Latto woke suddenly to see a short grey-haired man in his late fifties standing in front of him.

'I'm Tony Martinez, a detective with the Santa Cruz Police,' said the man, taking some paper from the inside pocket of his old brown jacket. He found a pen in a side pocket.

'Hello, Detective Martinez,' said Latto, starting to push himself up out of the chair.

Martinez stopped him by holding out a hand. 'Don't get up,' he said. 'I've just got a few questions for you.'

Latto sat uncomfortably on the front of the chair. Martinez took a seat on the sofa opposite. His grey trousers looked old. So did his shoes.

'Officer Seymour tells me you're British,' said Martinez.

'That's right,' replied Latto.

'So how is it that you know Ms Spencer?'

Latto thought for a moment before answering.

'I'm a doctor of western medicine and she's, she was, a doctor of Chinese, or Asian, medicine. She had some ideas that I was very interested in. We emailed each other about them. And then I came out here to learn more and so that she could teach me how to use these ideas on my patients.'

'So how well did you know her?' asked Martinez.

'Well, I met her once, a couple of years ago,' replied Latto. 'She was in London on holiday. We had dinner one evening. That's the only time we actually met. The rest of the time we just emailed each other.'

'And can you tell me what Ms Spencer was doing that interested you?'

Latto looked out of the window, deciding how to explain things to Martinez.

'You know what Parkinson's Disease is?' asked Latto.

'Sure. It's an illness that old people get. They shake a lot.'

Latto smiled.

'Actually it's not just old people who get it. Some young people get it too.'

'Oh! OK,' said Martinez.

'But you're right about the shaking,' continued Latto. 'Sometimes the hands and arms shake, sometimes the legs, sometimes both. It can do other things to the body too. Some people who have Parkinson's find it difficult to move parts of their body. Sometimes they can only move very slowly. Sometimes they find it difficult to move parts of their face. They can't smile. A lot of different things can happen to the body.'

Martinez was watching Latto and listening carefully. 'And what can you doctors do about it?' he asked.

'Well, western doctors can't do much really,' replied Latto. 'But Deborah was trying a new way of helping people who have this disease.'

'I see.' Martinez wrote something on the paper and then looked across at Latto again.

'When did you arrive in the States?' Martinez asked.

'Yesterday afternoon,' replied Latto. 'I got into San Francisco at about two o'clock and drove straight down here. Arrived about four thirty, five o'clock.'

'How long are you staying?' asked Martinez.

'Well, I was planning to stay for a couple of weeks. Now – I don't know.'

Martinez stood up.

'Well, you can't leave town just yet,' he said. 'Anyway, thanks, doc. That's it. You're free to go. On your way out tell Officer Seymour where you're staying. Oh – and ask me if you do want to leave town.' He took a card from the top pocket of his jacket and gave it to Latto. Latto stood up too.

'Can I ask you a question?' he asked.

Martinez nodded.

'How did she die?'

'We don't know yet,' said Martinez. 'We'll have to wait for the police scientists to have a look at her body.'

'But why are you here? I mean, you're a detective, aren't you?' asked Latto.

'I'm just checking to make sure everything's OK,' said Martinez. 'I mean, nobody's broken into the house. Nobody's been fighting in the house. She doesn't seem to have taken her own life.' Martinez put the paper away in his pocket. 'It looks as if she just died. I'm sorry, but sometimes it happens. Well, you must know that. You're a doctor.'

Latto thought about saying something, but decided not to. As a doctor, he knew that sometimes people did just die. A sudden heart problem or something like that. It happened, but it was unusual. And it was very unusual if the person was a healthy, happy forty-two-year-old woman, in a caring profession, and with everything to live for. For the second time that day he felt the hairs on the back of his neck stand up.

Chapter 2   *A robbery*

Latto was staying at the Ocean View Motel. It was on the side of a small hill opposite the end of the wharf. His room was halfway up the hill and looked out over the sea. It was a large room, with a double bed, a desk, a television and a cupboard. There was also a small kitchen and of course a bathroom. Outside his room there was a small plastic table and a couple of chairs. He could sit there in the sunshine and see the wharf and the beach.

Latto got back to his room about midday. He lay down on the bed and slept for a while. Afterwards he sat at the table outside his room, thinking about Deborah Spencer. He remembered her as a friendly and intelligent woman. She had been surprised that Latto, a doctor of western medicine, was interested in her work. But once she realised that his interest was serious, she was happy to share some of her ideas with him by email. It was terrible that she had died, and in such a strange way too. He hoped the police would find out what had happened.

Latto couldn't decide what to do about the next two weeks. He knew that Deborah Spencer worked with two other doctors in Santa Cruz – Ray and Sylvia. He knew their first names, but nothing else about them. Should he try and find them, and talk to them? He couldn't leave until Detective Martinez allowed him to, so it seemed like a good idea. Perhaps Martinez would know who these other doctors were. Latto could ask him tomorrow.

At about six o'clock Latto started to feel hungry. In front of his motel and right next to the end of the wharf was Casey's Bar and Grill. He had eaten there the evening before. It was a large friendly place, with good food and good service. Latto went in and was given a table by a window. He ordered a steak and a margarita. While he was eating, he thought back over the day and realised that he had left his sunglasses on the coffee table at Deborah Spencer's house. It was possible the police were still at the house so he decided to walk up there after he had finished his meal.

He left Casey's shortly after eight and started to walk up West Cliff Drive. The beach was empty, but out in the sea some of the sea lions that lived under the wharf were playing together. Latto climbed the hill past the Coast Santa Cruz Hotel and stopped when he reached Deborah Spencer's house. There was a white Dodge parked on the road in front of the house. Police scientists, thought Latto, probably still looking at things in the house.

The front door to the house was open a little, so Latto pushed it wide and walked in. Everything was quiet.

Latto called out, 'Hello!'

He stopped and listened for a few moments. There was no reply. He looked into the sitting room. There was no-one there. On the left of the front door was the dining room. That was empty too. Latto looked up the stairs. He thought he heard a noise.

Again he called out, 'Hello!' And he started up the stairs.

At the top, he stopped and listened again. Nothing.

There were four doors to choose from. The one on the left was half open and led into an office. Latto had just begun to move towards the door when suddenly it was thrown wide open and a young man almost ran out of the room. He looked angry. Under his left arm he was carrying a laptop computer, in his right hand was an empty plant pot.

'Who are you?' he asked, but he didn't wait for an answer. His right hand came up fast, flying towards Latto's head. By the time Latto realised what was happening it was too late. He was able to turn his head a little to the right, but not far enough. The plant pot hit the side of Latto's head hard and broke into pieces. Latto fell back and his head hit the wall with a sickening noise. His world went dark.

*   *   *

'Dr Latto. Are you OK? Hey! Wake up! Are you OK?'

Latto felt awful. His head felt as if it was full of small stones and they were all going round and round inside it. He opened his eyes to discover Detective Martinez looking down at him.

'Hey! Doc. Are you OK?'

'Do I look OK?' asked Latto.

Martinez smiled a little. 'Well, to tell you the truth, doc, you look terrible,' he said.

'Thanks.' Latto got to his feet with difficulty and brushed his clothes down with his hands. He moved slowly over to a mirror on the wall and looked in it as he felt his head very carefully.

'How does it feel?' asked Martinez.

'It hurts,' said Latto, 'but I think I've been quite lucky.'

'Good,' said Martinez. 'So, tell me, what happened?'

Latto met Martinez' eyes in the mirror.

'I left my sunglasses here this morning by mistake. I thought the police might still be here so I came back to get them. The front door was open and I walked in.'

'And?' asked Martinez.

'I called out a couple of times, but no-one answered. I was sure there was someone here because there was a car outside. I thought it must be the police scientists still working.'

'Right,' said Martinez, looking at Latto carefully.

'Well, I came up the stairs and someone came out of that room – the office, is it? – and hit me over the head with a plant pot.' Latto showed Martinez the pieces of pot. 'He probably found it in the room and picked it up to hit me with.'

Martinez took out some paper and a pen.

'Can you describe the person who did it?' he asked.

'I certainly can,' replied Latto. 'He was medium height, wearing old jeans, a black T-shirt and a baseball cap, and he had a gold ear-ring in his left ear.' Martinez took notes.

'He had a laptop under his arm,' Latto went on. Martinez made another note.

'I think he was on his own,' Latto added. 'I didn't see anyone else. Or hear anyone for that matter.'

Martinez pushed his fingers back through his hair.

'It's probably some kid,' he said. 'Some clever kid who saw the police cars earlier and realised the house was going to be empty tonight. Thought he could steal a few things and make a bit of money. You're at the Ocean View Motel, aren't you? I'll send someone round to show you some photos tomorrow afternoon. See if you can pick anyone out.'

'OK,' said Latto.

'Let me get a police car to take you to the hospital now so they can check you over,' said Martinez.

'Thanks,' said Latto, 'but I'll just walk back to my motel room. I'm OK. I just need to lie down. Some aspirin and some sleep is probably all I need.'

'OK,' said Martinez, laughing to himself a little. 'You're the doctor.'

As he walked back down West Cliff Drive, Latto thought about the man with the ear-ring. A death and then a robbery in the same house on the same day ... it couldn't just be chance.

Chapter 3   *Meeting the other doctors*

The following morning Latto woke up with a terrible headache. He took a couple of aspirin and made himself some coffee. He put on a light blue shirt and some jeans, and sat outside his room. As he looked down on the beach, he could see a few people already playing volleyball. Over to the right, in front of the Coast Santa Cruz Hotel, there were about twenty surfers out on their surfboards. Life here was very different. His hometown of Melrose in the south of Scotland was small compared to Santa Cruz. It wasn't by the sea and the weather was often cold and wet, especially at this time of year. He smiled to himself and thought about why he was here. There were people at home who needed him, patients with Parkinson's Disease who needed his help. At the moment that was far more important than sun, sand and surf.

Latto realised that he hadn't checked his email since he arrived. He went back into his room, got his computer out of his suitcase, started it up and got onto the internet. Emails were just starting to appear when there was a knock at the door. He went and opened it.

A young woman and an older, rather unhappy-looking man were standing outside. The woman spoke first.

'Mark Latto?' she asked.

'Yes.'

'Hi! I'm Sylvia Koning and this is Ray Molinaro.' She put out her hand. Latto shook hands first with her and then with Molinaro. Koning continued, 'We work, well, we worked with Deborah Spencer. She told us all about you. We've just been with Detective Martinez. He said you were staying here so we thought we should come along and introduce ourselves.'

Sylvia Koning was in her late twenties. She had long brown hair tied back, clear grey eyes and a nice smile. She was wearing dark blue trousers and a pink shirt. Ray Molinaro was probably in his late thirties. He was wearing a white T-shirt, jeans and light brown boots. He had thick black hair and there were dark circles under his eyes.

'Well, it's nice to meet you,' said Latto. 'Actually I was just trying to decide how to find you. Deborah talked about working with two other doctors. I knew you were called Ray and Sylvia, but she didn't tell me anything else about you. But then, I never thought …' Latto stopped talking. Nobody spoke for a moment. Then Latto said, 'It's a terrible business, her death, but … anyway, sorry, please sit down.'

They sat at the table outside Latto's room in the warm Californian sunshine.

'It's so sad about Deborah,' began Latto. 'Are the police saying any more about what happened?'

Molinaro spoke for the first time. He had a high, rather thin voice.

'Yes,' he said, 'the police scientists believe that Deborah had a heart problem and she just suddenly dropped dead. That's what Martinez told us this morning.'

'Strange,' said Latto, shaking his head. 'I only met her once a couple of years ago, but she seemed so healthy, so full of life.'

'She was,' said Koning. 'And it is strange – but sometimes these things happen.'

'Yes,' said Latto. 'True.'

It was quiet for a moment. Then Molinaro spoke. 'Detective Martinez said you'd had some trouble yourself last night.'

'That's right,' replied Latto, and started to explain about his visit to Deborah Spencer's house in the evening. As he described what had happened with the man with the earring, Koning's hand went up to her mouth.

'Oh no!' she said. 'Her laptop! The book! You say the man stole Deborah's computer?'

'What? Yes.' Not understanding, Latto looked from Koning to Molinaro and back.

'Deborah was writing a book,' explained Molinaro. 'It was a book about what we do: our work with our patients, what helps them, what doesn't help them, and so on.'

'Oh! I see,' said Latto. 'She hadn't told me that. But are you saying the book was on her computer?'

'Yes,' said Koning, 'and that was almost certainly the only copy.'

'But there must be other copies,' said Latto, 'on CD or paper.'

Molinaro shook his head. 'There aren't. She wanted to finish it first, then make copies for Sylvia and me to read. That's what she said. I told her to copy it onto a CD from time to time in case her computer broke down or someone stole it. But I'm sure she never did. She just didn't worry about things like that.'

Koning put her head in her hands. 'I can't believe it,' she said. 'All that work – just gone.'

Molinaro looked at his watch, then at Latto. 'I'm sorry,' he said. 'I've got to leave. I've got some patients waiting for me. Could I use your bathroom before I go?'

'Sure,' said Latto, and waved a hand towards the open door of his room. Molinaro stood up and went into Latto's room. Latto sat quietly, thinking that a lot of people, like Deborah Spencer, didn't keep copies of important things that they had on computer. Koning was looking out at the ocean and shaking her head slowly.

Latto looked at her and said, 'But you and Ray could write the book again, couldn't you?'

Koning shook her head. 'It would take years. Deborah knew so much more about how to help patients than either of us. We were still learning from her. All the time.'

Molinaro came back out of Latto's room. Hearing Koning's last words, he said, 'Deborah was our leader really – she started this new way of looking at the disease. Everything Sylvia and I know Deborah taught us. She was really the only person who could write about it.' Then, looking at his watch again, he said, 'I'm sorry. I really must go.'

Latto watched Molinaro walk down the stairs to the road, then he turned to Koning and asked, 'So Martinez didn't tell you someone had stolen the computer then?'

'No, he didn't,' replied Koning.

'So he doesn't know about the book?' asked Latto.

'Probably not,' said Koning. 'Why? Do you think it's important?'

'I don't know,' said Latto. He half closed his eyes in thought. 'It just all seems quite strange to me. Anyway, the police are coming round this afternoon to show me some photos. I'll tell them about the book and see what Martinez thinks about Deborah's death then.'

Chapter 4   *Talking to Martinez*

Sylvia Koning left a short time later, after she had agreed to meet Latto for dinner that evening. Latto went back into his motel room and woke up his computer. He looked at the emails that had come in: two from old friends, one from his bank, one from a neighbour in Britain, and then one from Deborah Spencer.

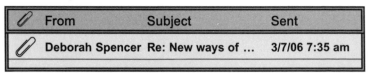

✎ From	Subject	Sent
✎ Deborah Spencer	Re: New ways of …	3/7/06 7:35 am

It had been sent the day he left Britain. He opened it quickly.

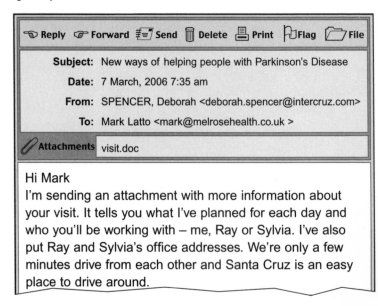

🔙 Reply   ☞ Forward   ✉ Send   🗑 Delete   🖨 Print   🚩 Flag   📁 File

Subject: New ways of helping people with Parkinson's Disease

Date: 7 March, 2006 7:35 am

From: SPENCER, Deborah <deborah.spencer@intercruz.com>

To: Mark Latto <mark@melrosehealth.co.uk >

Attachments visit.doc

Hi Mark
I'm sending an attachment with more information about your visit. It tells you what I've planned for each day and who you'll be working with – me, Ray or Sylvia. I've also put Ray and Sylvia's office addresses. We're only a few minutes drive from each other and Santa Cruz is an easy place to drive around.

Don't worry – I've also left you some free time to have a look at our beautiful California coast. You've got a free weekend when you could either visit San Francisco or go south to Monterey and Big Sur.
Looking forward to seeing you.

Ciao

Deborah

Latto opened the attachment and looked through it. The programme looked interesting. He felt sad though when he realised it was something he might never now be a part of. But maybe Sylvia and Ray would still share their ideas with him before he left. After all, that was why he had come here.

Sylvia and Ray's work addresses were there too, as promised. Latto found the map he had of Santa Cruz and made a note on it of their addresses. He closed the attachment, got off the internet and shut down his computer.

He looked at his watch. Twelve o'clock. His head was feeling a bit better. He was hungry, but he had to wait in for the police. He made a sandwich and took it outside to eat in the sunshine. After a few minutes Martinez appeared round the corner. He was carrying a laptop in one hand.

'It's a beautiful day and I wanted some fresh air so I came myself,' he explained, smiling. Then he waved a hand out towards the beach and the ocean. 'Nice place you found here.'

'Good, isn't it,' said Latto, pushing a chair out and inviting Martinez to sit down. 'I've got some cold beer in the fridge. Would you like one?' he asked.

'That's kind of you,' said Martinez, 'but I'm working. A glass of water would be good.'

Latto brought some water and then sat down next to Martinez. Martinez opened up the computer and handed it to Latto.

'A twenty-first-century book of photos,' he explained. 'Have a look through these. Press the "down" key to go to the next photo. Let me know if you see the man who hit you.'

'OK.' Latto started to look through the photos.

While Latto was doing this, Martinez spoke again. 'You were telling me about Parkinson's Disease,' he said. 'You were saying that western medicine can't do much for people who have it.'

'That's right,' replied Latto, continuing to look at the photos. 'We have a number of different drugs we can give people. The drugs can help the patient, but only for a few years. After that, the drugs stop working and the patient's condition will be the same as before. Maybe worse.'

Martinez thought about this for a few moments.

'Sounds bad,' he said.

'It is bad,' agreed Latto.

'So how were Ms Spencer's ideas different?'

'Well, I don't know too much about it yet – that's why I'm here,' said Latto, smiling at Martinez. 'However, it seems to work by holding the patient's arms and legs so that they have a chance to get better by themselves.'

Martinez looked thoughtfully at Latto.

'And this works?' he asked, looking surprised.

'For some people, yes, I believe so,' said Latto. 'For some people it's made a great difference.' He moved down to the last photo and then put the computer on the small table. 'I'm sorry,' he said. 'The man who hit me isn't one of these.'

'OK.' Martinez drank some water and looked out towards the beach and the wharf. Latto did too. There was a group of men and women making music on the beach – some of them playing guitars. There was a man with a snake round his shoulders walking past Casey's. This place is strange, thought Latto – surfers, people with snakes, sea lions living under the wharf.

'Those two other doctors – I told them where you were staying. Did they come round and see you earlier?' asked Martinez.

'Yes,' replied Latto. 'And I found out something interesting from them about Deborah Spencer's computer, the one that was stolen.'

'Oh yes?' said Martinez.

'Deborah was writing a book, putting down all her ideas about how to help people with Parkinson's Disease. And everything she had written was on that computer.'

'But she kept another copy somewhere?' said Martinez.

'The other doctors – Ray and Sylvia – they say she didn't. She … well, people don't always keep copies of things they should.'

'True,' said Martinez, looking carefully at Latto. 'So are you saying that this man with the ear-ring took the computer *because* Ms Spencer's book was on it?'

'It's possible,' Latto replied, 'but I don't know. I mean, maybe someone wanted to steal her ideas.'

'One of the other doctors?' asked Martinez.

Latto smiled. 'You're the detective,' he said.

Martinez laughed. 'Yes,' he said, 'I am. I think I'll find out a bit more about Ray and Sylvia. The scientists say it wasn't murder, but I always like to get the complete picture before I close a case.'

Chapter 5   *Dinner with Sylvia Koning*

That evening Sylvia Koning sat opposite Latto over the dinner table. She had changed into jeans and a shirt and had let her hair down around her shoulders. Latto thought she looked even prettier than before. Koning had chosen the restaurant, Giovanni's, on the wharf. The windows looked out towards the ocean. There were one or two late surfers still out on their surfboards.

Latto and Koning had had an excellent meal and were enjoying the last of a rich white wine from the Santa Cruz mountains. They had talked a bit about Latto's visit from Detective Martinez. But Latto said nothing about Martinez' plans to find out more about Ray and Sylvia. He hoped Martinez would find out nothing and Sylvia would never need to know. Latto asked about the work that Koning did with Parkinson's patients. By the time they moved on to coffee, they had started to find out more about each other's lives.

Koning told Latto how she had become a doctor, and about life in the town where she grew up with her parents and three brothers – Stowe, Vermont, in the east of the United States. They all skied a lot in the winter and went shooting and fishing in the summer. Latto told her about his life as a doctor in the small Scottish town of Melrose.

The conversation stopped and they were both quiet for a moment. Then Koning said, 'You're quite unusual, Mark, aren't you?'

'Are all Americans so direct?' asked Latto, smiling.

'My grandmother always taught me to say what I mean,' said Koning, laughing. 'But, no, you are unusual,' she went on. 'Not many doctors of western medicine are interested in anything that Asian medicine has to offer. I mean, I've been studying and practising Asian medicine for nearly ten years and you're the first doctor of western medicine to show any interest at all.'

'Really?' Latto searched for the right words to explain himself. 'It's probably in my blood though.'

Koning smiled and waited for him to continue.

'You see my father, his brothers and his sister, they all helped people in some way,' Latto continued. 'My father and his younger brother were doctors; my other uncle taught T'ai Chi and my aunt taught yoga.'

Latto caught the waiter's eye and asked for the bill.

'Interesting family!' said Koning.

'Well, yes,' agreed Latto, reaching for his wallet, 'so there were always a lot of ideas flying around, and a lot of healthy arguing. But that's probably why I'm so open to ideas from many different types of medicine. New ideas have always been a part of my life and my growing up.'

Latto paid and they left the restaurant to walk back along the wharf. It was beginning to get dark. Lights were on all along the seafront. However, the Boardwalk, the oldest seaside amusement park on the West Coast, was closed and quiet. During the winter months it was only open at weekends for children and their parents to enjoy the rides.

Latto and Koning walked slowly along. Then she looked at him. 'Is there a Mrs Latto?' she asked.

'So direct again,' said Latto, smiling and thinking to

himself that the evening might be more interesting than he had expected. 'No, there isn't. There isn't even a possible Mrs Latto at the moment.' He turned and looked down at Koning and they stopped walking.

'How about a Mr Koning?' he asked.

'No. No one,' said Koning. She smiled at him, then she turned and started walking again. Latto walked beside her. After a few steps she put her arm through his.

Towards the end of the wharf, Latto looked up towards the Ocean View Motel. He could see all the seafront rooms, one or two with lights on inside. He looked along until he found his room, the light off. Suddenly he saw something move. It was the window to his room. He stopped walking. Koning realised something was wrong.

'What's the matter?' she asked, looking up at him.

'There. My room.' They both looked up at the motel to see someone climbing out of Latto's window.

Latto was already moving, running along the wharf, shouting, 'Hey! Hey, you! Come back!' even though he was so far away the person wouldn't hear.

There was something under the robber's arm, but Latto couldn't see what it was.

Koning was running too, not far behind him. Latto reached the end of the wharf, ran round the entrance to Casey's Bar and Grill, across the road, and in through the entrance to the Ocean View Motel. He was too late – the robber had disappeared. The window of his room was still open. Koning came running up.

'It's no use, he's gone,' said Latto.

Latto unlocked the door and turned on the light. His suitcase was open on the bed. His computer was missing.

Over the next hour the police and the hotel manager arrived, followed shortly by Detective Martinez. He had heard the news on the police radio as he was driving home from a late meeting. Martinez called in the police scientists. The police spoke to the hotel manager, then to Latto and Koning. Detective Martinez spoke to Koning and then Latto. Nobody had any idea who the robber was but he, or possibly she, had taken Latto's computer and got away.

Koning went home, but before she did, she said goodbye to Latto, touching his arm and promising to call him in the morning. The hotel manager left. The police and the scientists left. Martinez had a few final words for Latto.

'Do you usually make this much trouble when you travel places?' he asked. 'You've only been here a couple of days. You arrive at a house with a dead body in it. Then someone hits you over the head with a plant pot. And now someone goes off with your computer. Are you always this lucky?'

They were standing outside Latto's room and in the half-light Latto wasn't sure if Martinez was joking or not. He decided to take a chance.

'A waiter once gave me too much change in a restaurant in Paris,' he said.

Martinez laughed.

'OK. Good one, doc. But seriously,' his voice changed, 'do you think someone might have wanted *your* computer rather than just any computer?'

'I've been thinking about that,' said Latto. 'But if so, I can't think why.'

'Of course,' continued Martinez, 'if it's a very new laptop, you could get about $500 for it on the street. That would buy a few drugs.'

Latto said nothing.

Martinez shook his head as if to clear his thoughts. 'Let's sleep on it,' he said. 'I've had a long day. I might be thinking better in the morning.'

Martinez left. Latto drank a beer and then went to bed.

As he lay waiting for sleep to come, he asked himself why someone might have wanted *his* computer. What could he have that might be of interest?

Then in the last few moments before he fell asleep, he realised what they wanted and how they had found out it was there. And he knew what he had to do in the morning.

Chapter 6   *Following Ray Molinaro*

At eight o'clock Latto woke to the sound of the sea lions under the wharf. He had a cup of coffee, then got out his map of Santa Cruz and checked where Ray Molinaro's office was. It was on Frederick Street, about five or ten minutes drive from the motel. The sun was up and it looked like being another fine day. Latto put on a yellow T-shirt and some old blue shorts. He put some water in a bottle to take with him and took his camera from the small cupboard beside his bed.

Latto found driving in California quite easy. OK, he was on the 'wrong' side of the road, but people drove slowly and carefully. Once downtown, Latto turned right onto Broadway, through an area of nice, well-kept houses. At the end of Broadway, he turned left onto Frederick Street. Molinaro's office was at the end of the street on the right, one of a number of offices beside the car park of the Dominican Hospital. Latto thought that Molinaro was probably nothing to do with the hospital, but that he just paid to use one of these offices.

It was eight thirty. There was no-one about. Latto parked his car and waited. He went back over the idea he had had last night before he fell asleep. He wanted to be sure it was right. He had just started to get his email yesterday morning when Koning and Molinaro had arrived. They had all sat outside, then Molinaro had gone into Latto's room. The computer was open on the desk so perhaps Molinaro saw that Deborah Spencer had sent him an email. Maybe he also saw that there was an attachment. He couldn't look at the email because Latto would know that someone had opened it. But he wanted to know what was in the attachment. So he, or someone he knew, had come back and stolen the computer. But why? Did Molinaro want to steal Deborah Spencer's ideas for himself? And if so, did Sylvia Koning know what was happening? Was she part of it too? Or was it really just someone who wanted money to buy drugs? Latto hoped Koning had no part in what was happening. She was an intelligent and interesting woman and he was beginning to like her.

Time passed. Latto wished he had brought a book or a newspaper. Then a white Dodge turned into the car park. It stopped outside Molinaro's office and a young man got out. He was wearing shorts and a T-shirt that said 'Surf Santa Cruz'. He was carrying a bag. He tried the door of Molinaro's office. Finding it locked, he went back to his car and put the bag back inside. Although he was wearing different clothes, Latto knew him from his ear-ring and baseball cap.

Standing next to his car, the man took a newspaper off the front seat and started to read it while he waited. Latto sat lower in his car seat, but the man didn't seem interested in any of the other cars in the car park. After a few minutes the man put his paper back on the front seat. Just then, a black Nissan turned into the car park and stopped next to the Dodge. Molinaro got out.

Molinaro and the man had a short conversation. Molinaro was wearing the same clothes as the last time Latto had seen him, but now he had a jacket over his T-shirt. During the conversation he reached inside his jacket, took out a thick envelope, and gave it to the man with the ear-ring. Latto had his camera ready and took photos. The man with the ear-ring reached into his car, took out the bag and gave it to Molinaro. Interesting envelope, thought Latto, just the right size for some money; and an interesting bag, just about the right size for my laptop. He took some more photos. The man got back in his car and drove off. Latto decided to stay with Molinaro.

Molinaro put the bag on the back seat of his car, locked his car and then walked over to his office. He went inside for a few minutes and then came out again. He got back into his car and drove off. Latto followed.

Molinaro drove out of Frederick Street and then out of town east on Highway 1. After Watsonville, he headed onto Highway 101 for Salinas. Soon he turned off again. Latto followed, keeping as far back as possible. A kilometre further on, Molinaro took a right turn and stopped in front of a large building. Latto drove past. A few hundred metres down the road he turned round and drove slowly back. Molinaro's car was parked out front. Molinaro was just going in through the front doors, the bag in his hand. Latto looked at the name on the building: Keiffenheim Laboratories Inc. Next to the name was a picture of two scientists in a laboratory. Both were wearing white coats. The first, a woman, was holding up a pill and looking at it carefully; the second, a man, was taking notes.

Latto drove on past and found his way back to Highway 1. He drove north back towards Santa Cruz. Molinaro might be in the building for hours. Latto didn't want to wait there. He needed to get back and speak to Martinez. He had information for him and some more questions. The most important one of all: what was a doctor of Asian medicine doing visiting a laboratory that made medicines used by western doctors?

Latto arrived back at his motel feeling hungry and thirsty. He had gone out without breakfast. He took a plastic bottle of orange juice out of the fridge. Before he opened it, a drop of juice appeared on the top of the bottle. He put down the bottle and the drop went away. He pressed the sides again, harder. A thin jet of juice shot out of the top. He looked carefully. There was a very small hole in the top of the bottle. He put the bottle down on the table, found Martinez' phone number and picked up the phone.

'Martinez. It's Latto. I'm at the Ocean View. I've got a big problem. I think you should come over here now.'

Chapter 7 *Problems*

Martinez arrived within fifteen minutes. Latto showed him the bottle of juice on the table.

'Watch this!' he said.

He reached down and slowly pressed the sides of the bottle. A few drops of juice came out of the small hole in the top.

'I was just about to open this bottle,' he explained.

Martinez didn't immediately understand.

'So you didn't make that hole?' he asked.

Latto shook his head.

'And it wasn't there when you bought the juice?' asked Martinez.

'I certainly didn't see it then,' Latto replied.

'So you're saying someone made this hole by putting something into the bottle of juice?' said Martinez.

'Yes,' said Latto. 'That's what I think.'

Martinez understood clearly now. 'I'll take the juice and get the scientists to check it.' He looked round the room. 'Perhaps the person who stole your computer last night did it.'

'Maybe,' said Latto. 'Or perhaps it was done this morning, while I was out. I went to Molinaro's office and —'

Just then Martinez' phone rang. Latto heard his side of the conversation: 'Yes … speaking … Yes, sir … but … Yes, that's true, sir … Yes, sir, I understand … Yes, I'll do that.' And then he finished the call. Throughout the call Martinez' face had grown dark, almost angry. He turned to Latto. 'Stay here. I'll be back in a minute.'

Martinez went down to the motel office; Latto waited outside his room. Martinez returned soon after, still not looking happy. They went into Latto's room and shut the door.

'Nobody saw anything this morning,' said Martinez. 'But the cleaners leave the doors open while they're cleaning the rooms. And sometimes they leave the rooms open while they go off to get fresh soap or shampoo or something. It's never for very long, but … How long did this person need?'

'Yes, not long,' agreed Latto.

Martinez sat down in a chair. Latto sat on the bed.

'OK, doc,' Martinez said. 'So now, to add to your problems, you think there's someone out there putting something in your orange juice. Trying to drug you, or even kill you. However, I've got a problem too now.'

Latto looked questioningly at Martinez.

'That was my boss on the phone earlier – Lieutenant Becker. He's taken me off the case.'

'What?' Latto couldn't believe it.

'The scientists say Ms Spencer wasn't murdered. I'm a homicide detective – in British English you'd say a murder detective – I'm not a robbery detective. Becker's given me the afternoon off and then I'm starting again tomorrow in Homicide. And someone else is going to look into the computer robberies – yours and Ms Spencer's.'

'But that's mad,' said Latto. 'The scientists could be wrong, and if someone is trying to kill me, that person could also be Deborah's murderer. Can't you say something to your boss? Can't you do something?'

There was a smile on Martinez' face, but not in his voice.

'Becker and I don't like each other much,' said Martinez, shaking his head. 'But even so, this is a bit of a surprise.'

Latto started to speak, but Martinez held up a hand.

'Just listen,' he said. 'You might be right that this is a murder case. However, I have to be very careful around Becker. There's nothing he'd like better than to make trouble for me.'

Martinez looked out of the window for a moment and then back at Latto.

'The good news is: I've got a free afternoon and evening so we've still got some time to look into your problem. The bad news is: I can't get help from the police department because I'm not on the case any more.'

'Well, thanks for staying with it, anyway,' said Latto.

Neither of them said anything for a moment. Then Martinez said, 'So why were you at Molinaro's office earlier?'

'I was doing some police work of my own,' Latto replied.

'Oh yes?' said Martinez.

'I think Molinaro wanted my computer,' Latto said and went on to explain everything.

'I think he saw that Deborah had sent me an email. And he thought the attachment to her email could be a copy of her book,' said Latto.

Martinez said nothing, but let Latto continue.

Latto described what he had seen outside Molinaro's office. He got out his camera and showed him the photos of Molinaro and the man with the ear-ring. 'I'm sure that's the man who hit me in Deborah's house,' Latto said. He went on to tell Martinez about his trip to Salinas and how Molinaro had taken his computer to Keiffenheim Laboratories. When he'd finished, he took the picture card out of his camera and gave it to Martinez.

'That's good work,' said Martinez, when Latto finished. 'You'd make a good detective.'

Latto smiled. 'It's not unlike being a doctor,' he said. 'A doctor looks at what's happening to a patient's body and works out what the illness is. A detective just looks at what's happening and works out who the criminal is.'

Martinez laughed. 'An interesting way of putting it,' he said. He pushed his fingers through his hair and looked at Latto as if deciding how much to tell him.

'I've been doing a bit of work myself,' said Martinez, 'finding out about those two who were working with Ms Spencer. There's nothing on Ms Koning yet. She's been here in Santa Cruz for eight years and she's not even got a parking ticket.' He looked Latto straight in the eye. 'But I have to say I'm never quite sure about people who are completely clean.'

'OK,' said Latto, hoping Martinez was wrong. 'And what about Molinaro?'

Martinez held up a finger. 'Ah,' he said. 'A different story.'

Chapter 8   *Martinez gets some answers*

Just then the phone in Latto's room rang. It was Sylvia Koning.

'I called you a couple of times earlier,' she said to Latto. 'Where have you been?'

Latto looked at Martinez. 'Oh, just enjoying Santa Cruz,' said Latto. 'How about meeting for dinner later?'

They agreed a time and Latto put down the phone. 'What about Molinaro?' he asked Martinez. 'You were starting to tell me about him.'

'Molinaro likes a game of cards,' he said. 'In fact he likes playing cards so much he goes to Las Vegas two weekends a month and plays in one of the casinos over there.'

Latto said nothing. He just let Martinez continue.

'The problem is that he really isn't very good at it. A friend of mine here in Santa Cruz told me Molinaro played cards. A friend of mine in Vegas told me the casinos are after him. He borrowed $150,000. Now he has to pay it back. And soon.'

'So Molinaro's short of money and he's in trouble,' Latto said slowly.

'What are you thinking?' asked Martinez.

There was quiet as Latto thought for a few moments more, then he spoke. 'Well, how about this? Drug companies are spending millions of dollars trying to find a way to help people with Parkinson's Disease, aren't they?' he explained.

Martinez had an interested look on his face.

'Now if a drug company found out that someone had

developed a way of helping people with Parkinson's Disease, or even, in fact, making them better, completely better, without using drugs, how are the drug company bosses going to feel?'

'They might well want to stop people finding out that information,' said Martinez.

'Right,' said Latto. 'They want people to buy their drugs. They don't want people to find out how to make themselves better without drugs.'

'So you're saying Keiffenheim Laboratories paid Molinaro to destroy Deborah's book?'

'Well, he does need money badly,' replied Latto.

'Seems possible to me,' said Martinez. 'I mean, Molinaro was in the right place to know when the book would be ready. He also had a good idea how many copies there were. Just the one – even though he'd told Ms Spencer it was a good idea to make more. If, of course, he did tell her that.'

'So what's next?' asked Latto.

'Well, we can't talk to Keiffenheim Laboratories – not yet anyway,' said Martinez. 'I'm sure a lot of doctors help them with their work, possibly even a few doctors of Asian medicine. And we don't know for sure that Molinaro has been doing anything wrong.'

'I'm sure,' said Latto quietly.

They sat for a moment or two, thinking about what they could do.

Then Latto said, 'One thing we need to know is who Molinaro talks to at Keiffenheim and how high up the company this person is. But we can't just ring Molinaro and ask him.'

Martinez smiled.

'Oh! I think we can,' he said. He took his phone out of one pocket and some papers out of the other. He looked through the papers. 'I've got Molinaro's number somewhere here,' he said.

He found the number. Latto listened to his end of the conversation.

'Hi. This is Charles Denning from California Telecom,' said Martinez, when the phone was answered. 'I'm calling from Keiffenheim Laboratories in Salinas. They've been having a lot of trouble with their phones and we're trying to put them right. People keep getting put through to the wrong extension. From the information I have here I see you've called them a few times in the last couple of weeks. Could you tell me what extension you've been calling? ... Yes, California Telecom ... That's right ... And did you have any problems getting through to the right extension? ... Sorry, what number was that again? ... Extension 342 ... OK ... No, that's fine ... Thank you very much, sir ... You have a good day now.'

Martinez finished the call. He reached for the phone book and opened it. He turned the pages, found what he wanted and got another number. 'Extension 342 ... Sorry, did you say Matthew Crocker's secretary ... OK, good ... Listen, my name's Carl Westlake. I met Matt last month and I'm just sending him a letter about some ideas we talked about. Could you tell me what he does in the company so I get it right when I write to him? ... He is ... OK, that's great ... Thanks very much ... Bye.'

Martinez turned to Latto with a smile on his face.

'Matthew Crocker, Head of Development,' he said.

Martinez put his phone in his pocket. 'Right,' he said, 'we

know who Molinaro talks to at Keiffenheim, but we don't know what they talk about. And we don't even know if Keiffenheim pays Molinaro money. We think we know – but we can't be sure. So where are we now? We need a plan.'

'I've got a plan,' said Latto.

Chapter 9   *Catching Crocker*

Latto and Martinez went through the plan carefully. When they reached agreement, Martinez went out to his car and came back with an MP3 recorder. He joined it up to the motel room phone. Latto picked up the phone.

'Matthew Crocker, please,' he said when it was answered.

Crocker's secretary wanted to know his name and his business.

'Tell Mr Crocker it's Dr Mark Latto calling. And I want to speak to him about a book – a book to help patients who have Parkinson's Disease.'

Crocker was on the line in less than thirty seconds.

'What can I do for you, Dr Latto?'

Latto smiled to himself. 'I think it's more a question of what I can do for you,' he said.

'Really?' Clearly Crocker wanted to find out how much Latto knew.

'I believe I have a copy of a book you're interested in,' said Latto.

'I don't know what you're talking about,' replied Crocker. His voice didn't sound worried at all.

'I understood you were interested in copies of a book about helping Parkinson's patients.'

'What makes you think that?' asked Crocker.

'Don't play games, Crocker,' said Latto, his voice becoming hard. 'You know Ray Molinaro. You *are* interested in this book. And I have a copy.'

'I think not, Dr Latto,' said Crocker. 'I am told there are no copies left.'

'I'm afraid you'll find that you've got some wrong information there,' explained Latto. 'As you probably know, I came over to California to see Deborah Spencer. Well, just before I came, she emailed me a copy of her book. She asked me to read it before I came.'

'Really?' said Crocker. 'How interesting!' His voice didn't sound interested. Latto began to worry.

'Of course I copied the book onto CD. I don't keep things like that on my computer,' he continued. 'And anyway, my computer unfortunately got stolen – but, of course, I've still got the book on CD.' Latto said nothing for a moment so that Crocker had time to consider what he had said. Then he spoke again. 'I'm sure I can find another buyer, if it's not of interest to you.'

No-one said anything for what seemed like minutes. Martinez watched Latto closely.

Then Crocker spoke. 'Can I call you back, Dr Latto?'

'No,' said Latto. 'I'll call you. Five minutes. No longer.' He put the phone down.

Latto took out a handkerchief to dry his hands.

'He's calling Molinaro to check that it's possible you have a copy,' explained Martinez.

'Sure,' said Latto.

'You've also got to make him believe that you want to sell it,' said Martinez. 'It might seem strange to him. I mean, you come here to see Ms Spencer and find out about her work so that you can help people with Parkinson's Disease. But now you want to sell the key to her work – without finding out how you can help those people.'

Latto nodded, looking thoughtful. They waited, saying nothing.

After a few minutes Latto looked at his watch and picked up the phone again.

'I'm not sure why you want to sell this book,' said Crocker when he came on the line. 'Or, in fact, why you think I might want to buy it.'

This is like fishing, thought Latto. I'm holding out a piece of bread and waiting for the fish to bite. I'm giving him what he wants and I have to make him think it's OK – it's not going to hurt him.

'I'm selling it for the money,' said Latto. 'That's easy. Sure, I was interested in what Deborah Spencer had to say. But at that time I didn't know how valuable her ideas were, how much they were worth to you. I mean, with the $150,000 you're going to pay me, I'll be able to start my own health centre back home.'

There was a laugh at the other end of the line.

'Dr Latto, if you think I'm going to pay $150,000 for your CD, you're making a big mistake.'

'I think you're wrong there,' said Latto. 'I mean, think about how much your company earns from the anti-Parkinson's drugs you sell at the moment. And think about how much you are spending on the development of new drugs. Well? $150,000 is nothing.'

Crocker said nothing. He was being very careful.

'How will I know it's the only CD you made?' he asked.

'You won't,' replied Latto. 'You'll just have to believe me. $150,000 is all I want. Once I get it, I'll be off back to Britain.'

Crocker said nothing.

Latto waited a few moments, then he said, 'Well, do we have an agreement?'

'I need to think about this,' said Crocker.

'You've got ten seconds,' said Latto.

Crocker only needed five.

'OK,' he said. 'We have an agreement.'

'Right,' said Latto. '$150,000. Old notes. Tonight ...'

'Tonight! Impossible,' began Crocker.

'Tonight is possible,' said Latto. 'If not, I'll take the CD somewhere else. We'll meet at the University of Santa Cruz arboretum.'

'The what?' asked Crocker.

'Arboretum – it's like a garden, a very big one, but it has trees in it which the university use for study. I was out there yesterday afternoon. It'll be nice and quiet at night.'

Meeting at the arboretum had been Martinez' idea. Late at night it would be empty, and Martinez could get them in.

'I don't know where it is,' said Crocker. 'I've only been to Santa Cruz a couple of times.'

'Find it,' said Latto. 'You want the CD. You find it. Make sure you come alone – that's important. And bring the money. The arboretum will be open. Come inside and walk up the hill in front of you. Walk round to the left and you'll see an open-air theatre down to your left. Go down there and wait for me. Midnight.'

'I can't get $150,000 by midnight.' Crocker sounded angry.

'Of course you can,' said Latto. 'You work for a large company that makes medicines all over the world. Don't tell me you can't find $150,000 when you need it. Midnight. Don't be late.'

Latto put the phone down.

Martinez stood up and put a hand on Latto's shoulder.

'Good work, doc,' he said. 'I'll go and pick up one or two things we'll need. I'll be back about eleven o'clock.'

Chapter 10   *Meeting Crocker*

At 10.45 that evening Latto and Sylvia Koning climbed the steps from the street up towards Latto's room in the Ocean View Motel. They had had dinner at Casey's, talking about films and books they liked, places they had visited, people they knew – everything, thought Latto, except the last two days. It had been a lovely evening, but Latto couldn't help thinking about what Martinez had said. Martinez must be wrong, he thought. Koning couldn't know anything about what was going on.

As they reached the top of the steps, Martinez came round the corner. Seeing Sylvia Koning, he looked questioningly at Latto.

'Hi, Martinez,' said Latto. 'We've just been having dinner.' He turned to Koning, taking her hand in his. 'Listen, Sylvia,' he said. 'I'm sorry, but I've got to go and help Martinez for an hour or so. Do you want to wait here in my room and we can have a drink or something when I get back? Or I could meet up with you tomorrow?'

Koning looked from Latto to Martinez and back. If she felt surprise, she kept it out of her voice. She just put her arms round Latto and pulled him close.

'Don't be long,' she said. 'I'll wait here.'

'OK.' Latto gave her his key. 'We'll be an hour – two at the most.'

Latto and Martinez walked up to the car park, got into Martinez' Jeep Grand Cherokee and drove off. They didn't see Koning run to her Suzuki soft-top, jump in and follow them out.

As Latto and Martinez turned left into 2nd Street, Martinez spoke. 'I found out something interesting about Crocker.'

'Oh yes?' replied Latto.

'He goes to the same boat club as my boss, Becker.'

'Interesting,' said Latto.

'Yes, I thought so too,' agreed Martinez.

The drive to the arboretum only took about ten minutes. Martinez stopped the car just outside the gates and got out. He took a large key out of his pocket and opened the gates. He drove inside and parked behind a tree on the left of the entrance. Then he got out and closed the gates again, but didn't lock them.

There was a full moon so it wasn't too difficult to see what they were doing. Martinez opened the back door of his car and started taking things out. First he took out two guns. He put one in his jacket pocket and offered the other to Latto.

'Here, take this,' said Martinez.

'No, thanks,' said Latto.

'Come on. Crocker's sure to have one,' said Martinez.

'I'd really prefer not to,' replied Latto.

'OK.' Martinez didn't look happy about it. 'It's up to you.' Next he took out a small microphone and put it just inside the front top pocket of Latto's jacket.

'That's the microphone,' he explained. 'I'll be able to hear all of your conversation. And, of course, I'll record it as well.' He showed Latto the recorder on the back seat of the car. Then he took a second microphone and hid it inside the front of Latto's jacket.

'If he searches you and finds one microphone, he'll probably think that's all there is.'

'OK,' said Latto.

Martinez gave Latto a torch and took one for himself. Then he took the recorder out of his car and closed the back door. Turning on their torches, they started up the hill. They passed a small wooden building on their left. Latto's torch lit up some information on the side of the building. He read, 'Danger – Mountain Lions'. Below that it told you what to do if you met a mountain lion.

'Don't worry about that,' said Martinez. 'Lions come out of the countryside into the arboretum all the time, but we'll be staying close to these buildings. They won't come down here.'

At the top of the hill, Martinez looked down and to the left.

'The theatre's down there,' he said. 'You wait for Crocker there. Remember – get him talking when he arrives. When I think he's said enough, I'll come out.'

'Where will you be?' asked Latto.

'Over there, behind those trees. I'll keep well hidden until I've heard enough,' replied Martinez.

Latto found an old chair in the open-air theatre and sat down. He looked at his watch. He had twenty minutes to wait. Time passed slowly. Latto thought back over the last three days. It all seemed completely unreal. Three days ago he had set off from Britain to find a new way to help some of his patients. Now he was trying to catch a man who had ordered a number of crimes, possibly including murder.

Shortly before midnight, Latto heard a sound. Then there was quiet. Complete quiet for a long time. Suddenly there was a noise behind him. Latto stood up and turned round. A man was standing there, a gun in one hand, a bag in the other.

'Matthew Crocker?' asked Latto.

'Yes.'

'I don't think there's any need for that,' said Latto, nodding at the gun. 'I had hoped we could do this without guns.'

'Sit down,' ordered Crocker. His voice sounded ugly.

'I hope you're not thinking you can kill me as well,' said Latto.

'Where's the CD?' asked Crocker.

Latto put a hand against his side pocket.

'Let's see it,' said Crocker.

Latto took a CD case slowly from his pocket. 'Where's the money?' he asked.

'Here.' Crocker put the bag on the ground.

'Could you open it, please,' said Latto. 'I'd like to see it.'

'How do I know that's the only CD?' asked Crocker once more.

'I told you. You don't,' replied Latto. 'You'll just have to believe me when I say it is. You should realise that I don't want to end up like Deborah Spencer, so you'll find I'm telling the truth.'

'Throw it over here,' said Crocker.

'The money,' said Latto.

Keeping his gun on Latto, Crocker went down on one knee and opened the bag. It was full of US bank notes. He stood up again. He moved away from the bag.

'Throw the CD over here and you get the money,' he said.

Latto threw the CD. Crocker picked it up and put it in his pocket.

Latto moved towards the money.

'Stop!' Crocker's voice was hard and loud.

There was a noise from the top of the hill. Latto saw

someone in the moonlight, coming down towards them. As the person came closer he realised who it was. The man with the ear-ring.

'All clear,' he said to Crocker.

'Thanks, Max,' said Crocker. He looked at Latto again. 'I'm glad to hear that you came alone, Dr Latto. However, I'm afraid this is the end for you.'

Chapter 11   *A surprise appearance*

Martinez has heard all this, thought Latto. But had Crocker said enough? At the moment Crocker clearly thought all his problems were over: he had the CD and, as far as he knew, he had the only person who knew about it. Perhaps now he would say more about what happened to Deborah Spencer.

'Would I be right in thinking that you ordered Deborah Spencer's death?' asked Latto.

'You Brits!' Crocker laughed. 'Such correct English. "Would I be right in thinking ..."' His voice became hard. 'Yes, you would be right. I ordered her death. We've spent hundreds of millions of dollars looking for new medicines for Parkinson's Disease and I wasn't going to see that money thrown away. I wanted her out of the way and I wanted her notes, her book, destroyed. I thought everything had gone really well, but unfortunately she sent you a copy. Unlucky for you really.'

Crocker smiled. It wasn't a nice smile. Max was now standing beside Crocker. He was smiling too.

'Did you use one of Keiffenheim's drugs to kill her then?' asked Latto. Crocker seemed happy to talk.

'Actually we did,' he said. 'Cloperoxomine. It's usually given to people with weak hearts. But if you give too much to anyone, it stops their heart. It doesn't matter if they have a weak heart or a strong heart. Cloperoxomine stops it. Also it disappears very quickly in the blood. If the scientists don't know what they're looking for, it's difficult to find.'

'Clever,' said Latto. 'So that's what Max put in my orange juice, was it?'

Crocker's mouth dropped open.

'How do you know about that?' he asked.

Just then another noise came out of the darkness. At last, thought Latto, Martinez has decided to come out.

But then Crocker spoke: 'Ah! Ray, I see you found someone hiding among the trees.'

Latto turned to see Martinez coming down towards him. He was looking angry. His hands were behind his head. Molinaro was holding a gun to his back. In Molinaro's other hand was the recorder.

'He was over there behind the trees,' said Molinaro, 'listening to everything and recording it on this.' He waved the recorder in the air and then threw it on the ground near Crocker. 'This was in his pocket too.' Walking round to stand next to Crocker, he took Martinez' gun from his own pocket and passed it to Crocker.

'Well, well, well,' said Crocker. 'You must be Detective Martinez. I was talking to Lieutenant Becker about you only this afternoon.'

Crocker turned back to Latto. 'Once again you've tried to be too clever, Dr Latto.' He looked quickly at Molinaro. 'Search him,' he said, nodding at Latto. 'He may have a gun on him. Find the microphone too.'

Molinaro came over to Latto. Careful to keep Latto between himself and Crocker, Molinaro searched him. He found both the microphones, and threw them to Crocker.

'Not just one microphone – but two.' Crocker smiled and shook his head. He dropped them both on the ground and broke them by standing on them.

Latto looked round. Crocker had given Martinez' gun to Max so all three of them had guns. It looked hopeless.

'Wait a minute,' said Latto, quickly trying to think of something to stop Crocker. 'I think you should know that CD wasn't really the only copy I made of the book.'

Crocker laughed. 'Too late, Dr Latto. Too late. I believed you the first time. You already know how dangerous I can be. I don't believe you kept another copy.' He laughed again, then looked round at the three of them. 'I just want to sort out this problem and forget about you. Ray, Max, you know what to do. I don't mind where the police find their bodies. It's probably best to throw them in the sea when you've killed them. It'll make life a bit more difficult for the police scientists. Throw that recorder in the sea too.'

Latto looked at Martinez, hoping that he would say something. But Martinez was just looking straight at Crocker, his face dark and angry.

Latto tried again. 'Look, Crocker, I'm sure you don't have to —'

'Shut up!' Crocker's voice was angry. 'Kill them,' he said to Max and Molinaro.

He picked up the bag with the money in. Putting his gun in his pocket, he started to walk away from the group up the hill, and out of the open-air theatre.

He had only taken a few steps when a voice shouted, 'Drop your guns and don't move!'

Chapter 12 *Guns and mountain lions*

Crocker stopped and looked round. So did everyone else. They couldn't see anyone. No-one knew where the voice had come from. Then Crocker moved, his hand going towards the pocket where he had put his gun. There was the sudden loud noise of a shot. Crocker screamed and dropped the bag. Everyone moved at the same time.

Latto turned quickly and, knocking Molinaro's gun hand to one side, hit him hard in the stomach. Molinaro fell forwards and Latto hit him again on the back of the head. Molinaro fell to the ground and lay there without moving.

It took Martinez only a few seconds to reach Crocker. Crocker was in no condition for a fight. The shot had hit his left hand and there was blood all over it. It clearly hurt. Martinez pushed him to the ground, face down, and pulled Crocker's good hand halfway up between his shoulders. Then, holding him down with one hand, he used his free hand to take Crocker's gun from his pocket. That done, he moved back a few metres and kept a careful watch over Crocker and Molinaro.

Max had already disappeared. He had turned and run when he heard the shot. Latto saw someone else running past him and after Max. He picked up Molinaro's gun and followed.

Max was quick. He led the way up through the trees. The person following wasn't far behind, and Latto was a few metres behind them. It was easy to find their way in the moonlight. They passed the South African Garden and the New Zealand Garden. Max ran faster, got about twenty metres ahead and then quite suddenly disappeared into some trees. Everything went quiet.

Latto and the person in front of him both stopped. Latto moved forward slowly to see who it was. Long brown hair tied back.

'Sylvia! What are you doing here?' He couldn't believe his eyes.

'Sh!' said Koning. She kept her eyes on the trees ahead. There were noises in the trees. Far off there was a loud animal noise; then another one closer to where they were standing.

'Mountain lions,' said Koning.

'Are they dangerous?' asked Latto.

'They can kill,' said Koning. Then without turning her head, she asked Latto, 'This man in the trees – the one with the ear-ring – do you know his name?'

'Max.'

Koning called out, 'Hey, Max! There are mountain lions out there. Do you want one of them after you? Or you can come with us. Just come out and throw down your gun.'

There were more noises and then suddenly Max appeared from the trees. He was running towards them as fast as he could. Behind him was a mountain lion, getting nearer with every step.

Koning went down on one knee, looking along her gun. Seconds passed as she waited for the right moment. Then she shot. The mountain lion took one more step and fell to the ground like a stone.

Koning was immediately back on her feet, her gun pointing at Max.

'Stop!' she ordered loudly. 'And drop your gun!'

Max did what he was told.

*　　　*　　　*

As they arrived back at the open-air theatre, Martinez was speaking into his phone.

'I need a van over here and five or six officers. There are two ...' – he looked up and saw the others arriving back – '... no, three men here to take to jail, though one probably needs the hospital first.' He finished the call and turned to Koning.

'Not a bad shot,' he said.

'She just killed a lion back there,' said Latto.

'I did tell you.' Koning smiled. 'I used to go shooting a lot in the summer back home.'

Crocker was sitting on the ground, holding a handkerchief round his bloody hand. Latto walked over and looked down at him. He reached down, felt in the side pocket of Crocker's jacket and pulled out the CD. He held it in front of Crocker's face.

'This is what caught you, Crocker. Do you want to know what it really is? It's a CD of some bad country music that one of my patients gave me before I came to Santa Cruz. There are no copies of Deborah Spencer's book.' He waved a hand at Crocker, Max and Molinaro. 'You and your friends took care of that. But at least we made sure you'll all go to prison.' He looked at Martinez. 'Right, Martinez?'

'Right,' replied Martinez.

Crocker had a strange look on his face as he listened to Latto. It turned into a kind of half-smile and he said, 'Well, at least nobody will be reading Deborah Spencer's book in the future, even if I am in jail. Keiffenheim Laboratories will be very happy.'

Just then blue lights appeared as three police cars drove in through the gates and up the hill to the top of the open-air theatre.

Chapter 13   *Who killed Deborah?*

'Molinaro's told us everything,' said Martinez, looking round at Latto and Koning. They were all sitting outside Latto's room at the Ocean View Motel.

It was ten o'clock in the morning. Latto and Koning had got back some time before. Martinez had joined them for breakfast at Casey's. Now they were sitting in the sunshine talking about what had happened the night before.

'So was it Ray?' asked Koning. 'Did he kill Deborah?'

'Yes,' said Martinez. 'He says Crocker ordered him to do it, so we're holding Crocker for murder too.'

'But Molinaro gave her the Cloperoxomine?' Latto asked.

'Yes,' replied Martinez. 'The scientists are going to have another look at Deborah Spencer's body. But from what Crocker told you I don't know whether they'll find anything. However, Molinaro has told us everything. He put the drug in some milk in her fridge. It was just a matter of time before she drank it.'

'You know, I can't believe that Ray could do that,' said Koning. 'He was such a caring doctor. His patients really liked him.'

Martinez looked at Latto. 'We think it was Max who tried to kill you the same way. It seems that your detective work wasn't so good after all. Molinaro saw you when you followed him down to Salinas, though only as he arrived at Keiffenheim Laboratories. He told Crocker, Crocker phoned Max, and Max came round here and put Cloperoxomine in your orange juice. I haven't heard back from the scientists yet, but I'm sure that's what we'll find in it.'

'But why did Crocker agree to meet me?' asked Latto. 'He thought I would soon be dead and he thought I had a CD of the book. With me dead, all he had to do was come here and get the CD.'

'The problem was he didn't know when you would die,' explained Martinez. 'He really believed you had the CD when you spoke to him on the phone. He didn't want the police to find you first and take all your things to the police station – including the CD. He wanted it. With Deborah Spencer it was easier. Again Crocker didn't know when she would die. But once the police had finished at her house, he could send Max round later to get her laptop.'

'So Crocker ordered Deborah's death so that he could steal her book and save his company millions of dollars,' said Latto.

'That's about it,' said Martinez.

'Poor Deborah.' Koning put her hands to her face, sad at the thought of her friend's death. 'How can people think money is worth more than a person's life?' she asked. Nobody answered.

They sat quietly for a few moments.

Then Latto asked, 'What about Becker?'

Koning looked questioningly at him and he quickly explained how Crocker and Martinez' boss knew each other.

'He's in the clear at the moment,' said Martinez. 'I know Crocker said something about him out at the arboretum, but it was after we'd stopped recording. And Crocker's not saying much at all now. You have to remember that Becker's my boss. I have to be very sure before I say anything against him.'

Then he laughed. 'But I'm watching him very carefully now.'

When Martinez had gone, Latto and Koning stood and looked down towards Casey's and the ocean.

Latto put his arm around Koning's shoulders. He tried to put his feelings into words. She really hadn't known what Crocker and Molinaro were doing. Martinez had been wrong and he had been right. After what she had done out at the arboretum, Latto felt happy, thankful and very close to her. He looked down at her and said, 'Tell me – why exactly did you follow us out to the arboretum?'

Koning smiled. 'I told you I had three brothers. I know what boys get up to late at night. It usually means trouble.'

Latto laughed.

'I know it might not seem like it after the last three days,' said Koning, 'but Santa Cruz is really a great place to be.' She looked up at him. 'And, even though I'm not Deborah, I can still show you some new ways to help people with Parkinson's Disease.'

Latto smiled. 'Great,' he said. 'In fact I was hoping you'd say something like that. But remember, Deborah also made sure I had some free time in my programme.'

Koning looked into his eyes, then she stood on her toes and kissed him softly.

'Perhaps we ought to make a start with some free time,' she said.

Chapter 14 *Ten days later*

Latto stayed in Santa Cruz for the whole two weeks after all. He and Sylvia Koning spent that time together. He watched her at work and she showed him how Deborah Spencer had taught her to help patients with Parkinson's Disease. They spent evenings and nights together at her house near Twin Lakes State Beach. They took time off and travelled down to Monterey and Big Sur for the weekend. They tried not to think about the time when Latto would return to Scotland.

On Latto's last evening, he and Koning were sitting outside his room, drinking beer and looking over the ocean. Suddenly Martinez appeared carrying a bag in each hand.

'Your laptop,' he said, giving one of the bags to Latto. 'The Salinas police found it at Crocker's house. The scientists have finished with it and I thought you might like it back before you go home.'

'Thanks,' said Latto.

'It might be a good idea to check it still works,' said Martinez. 'But before you do that, take a look at this.'

The door to Latto's room was open. Martinez walked in and put the other bag on the desk. He took out another laptop and started it up. Latto and Koning had followed Martinez into the room and were watching him.

'This is Deborah Spencer's laptop,' Martinez explained. 'I thought you might like to see this email that came in a couple of days ago. You might even want to note down the address of the person who sent it.'

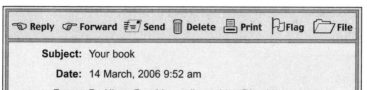

Subject: Your book

Date: 14 March, 2006 9:52 am

From: Dr Alison Partridge <ali.partridge@healthcan.ca>

To: SPENCER, Deborah <deborah.spencer@intercruz.com>

Attachments

Dear Deborah

I was so pleased to get the copy of your book that you emailed me last week.

I've read it all through and I think it's really interesting. Of course, there have been developments in the drugs industry. The drugs that are given to people with Parkinson's Disease are getting better all the time. However, your way of looking at the disease is so completely new and different.

I've got lots of questions to ask, but I'm coming down to San Francisco in a couple of weeks on business. Perhaps I could come down to Santa Cruz and meet up with you then? I'd be able to come down on March 30 or 31. Which date would be best for you?

By the way, I got an email from Gina last week. I haven't heard from her in about fifteen years! Do you remember her? She was the very tall one in our class at UCLA. I'll tell you all about it when I see you.

With best wishes – and congratulations

Love

Ali

Cambridge English Readers

Look out for these other titles at Level 3:

Eye of the Storm
by Mandy Loader

A hurricane is tearing across the Atlantic from the west coast of Africa towards the USA. As the hurricane passes through the Caribbean, it destroys everything in its path. In Florida, a man is out in a fishing boat, unaware of the approaching disaster. His daughter, Ikemi, and her boyfriend must confront the hurricane in a desperate attempt to reach her father before it is too late.

Double Cross
by Philip Prowse

A fast-moving international thriller set in Scandinavia, London and southern Africa. A politician nearly dies in Stockholm, and secret agent Monika Lundgren chases the would-be killer. As she races across the world she meets a strange football team, a rock musician, and a madman with dreams of world power.

The House by the Sea
by Patricia Aspinall

A married couple, Carl and Linda Anderson, buy a house by the sea to spend their weekends. But one weekend Linda does not arrive at the house and Carl begins to worry. What has happened to her? Who is the taxi driver that follows Carl? And how much do the people in the village really know?

www.cambridge.org/elt/readers